S T O W A W A Y

Written and directed
by Hannah Barker and Lewis Hetherington

Douglas!

Thanks so
much for
supporting me
& the Show!

(LEWIS)

Stowaway was first performed at New Wolsey Theatre, Ipswich on 18 September 2014. The revised version was first performed at Platform, Glasgow on 19 February 2016.

Cast

Aditya	Devesh Kishore
Andy	Steven Rae
Debbie/Salma	Balvinder Sopal
Lisa	Hannah Donaldson

Creative and Production Team

Directors and Writers	Hannah Barker and Lewis Hetherington
Designer	Rhys Jarman
Lighting Design	Katharine Williams
Sound Design and Music	Philip Pinsky
Movement Director	Kane Husbands
Production Manager	Helen Mugridge
Stage Manager	Ian Smyth
Stage Manager	Molly Stoker
Costume Supervisor	Verity Sadler
Set Builder	Pablo Cattermole
Producer	Ric Watts
Production Photographer	Richard Davenport
Graphic Designer	Liam Jarvis

An Analogue production in association with New Wolsey Theatre. National tour produced in association with Platform. Supported by Arts Council England, Creative Scotland and British Council Developed at National Theatre Studio, Traverse Theatre and Shoreditch Town Hall.

Analogue would like to say a special thanks to Tom Green at Counterpoints Arts, Emily Churchill Zaraa at Migrants Resource Centre and Ashvin Devasundaram, Gulwali Passerlay, Hasan Abdalla and Maryam Hashemi for their stories and input which made a huge difference to the writing and making of this show. Thanks to those we met in India – Lasya Mavillapalli, Lavanya Mavillapalli, the Narasimhacharis and the rest of Team Rasoham (Chennai); and Vikram Iyengar, Debashree and the rest of Ranan (Kolkata). Thanks to Taqi Nazeer, Alexandra Maher, Vanessa Cook and Helen Fagelmen for their brilliant work during the 2014 pilot tour, and to Joseph Arkley, Selina Boyack, Finn den Hertog, Scott Hoatson, John McKeever, Adura Onashile, Tom Peters, Caroline Valdes and the New Wolsey Young Company for invaluable contributions during the show's development. Thanks to Nirnal Sopal (for the translation); Ice and Fire; Refugee Council; Malcolm Stephen; Sarah Belcher; Andy Clark; Nick Walker; Andrew Mills; Iain Craig; Alex Markham; Playwrights' Studio Scotland; and Gavin and Fiona at Farnham Maltings. Plus special thanks to our project partners – Sarah, Rob, Paul, Ed and all at New Wolsey Theatre; Matt and the team at Platform; Nick, James and all at Shoreditch Town Hall; and all at Traverse Theatre, Arts Council England, British Council and National Theatre Studio.

www.analoguetheatre.co.uk

Analogue makes ambitious new theatre inspired by real stories and contemporary ethical questions. We collaborate with a wide network of pioneering thinkers to bring together research and invention and create performance that fuses the real with the imagined, the human with the scientific.

We are particularly excited by the possibilities of documentary, neuroscience, interactivity and new technologies and strive to continue to cross boundaries of continents and disciplines, embracing national and international arts organisations and audiences.

Analogue, formed in 2007, is an associate company of Farnham Maltings, and has produced a number of award-winning and critically acclaimed shows, including: *Mile End* (2007), *Beachy Head* (2009), *Lecture Notes on a Death Scene* (2010), *2401 Objects* (2011), *Re-enactments* (2013) and *Transports* (2014).

Analogue's work regularly tours the UK, and increasingly is being developed through international collaboration. Our work ranges in form and scale from stage-shows to audio tours, multi-platform experiences and intimate, interactive performances.

Analogue is an on-going collaboration between co-directors Hannah Barker & Liam Jarvis, Producer Ric Watts, Production Manager Helen Mugridge and Associate Artist Lewis Hetherington, working with collaborators from fields as diverse as neuroscience, social-psychology, pervasive media, computer aided modelling, movement, performance, scenography and playwrighting.

Analogue is an Associate Company of Farnham Maltings, where the company is currently administratively based, and Shoreditch Town Hall. Between 2010-12, we were also an Affiliate Company at the National Theatre Studio.

'Bright young things of British Theatre'
The Observer

HANNAH BARKER

Hannah is a writer, director, facilitator and theatre-maker. She co-found Analogue, an award-winning theatre company creating new work inspired by real stories. Trained in theatre and as a journalist, Hannah has co-written and directed the company's work including *Mile End* (Fringe First 2007, Arches Brick Award 2007); *Beachy Head* (Critically acclaimed); *2401 Objects* (Fringe First 2011) co-produced by Staatstheater Oldenburg, and *Stowaway* (2016 UK tour). She is currently co-writing *Sleepless*, co-produced by Staatstheater Mainz and *Transports*, an interactive experience exploring Parkinson's disease, piloted at the Science Museum in 2014. Analogue's work has been published by Oberon, with two more plays due for release in 2016. Hannah facilitates workshops and creates new shows with young people, including on *The Tomorrow Project* at the Donmar Warehouse, Derby Theatre, Playbox, The Brit School, Central School of Speech and Drama and Shakespeare Schools Festival.

HANNAH DONALDSON

Recent theatre credits include *Lifeboat*, *The Voice Thief* (Catherine Wheels); *Happy Hour*, *The Yellow Wallpaper* (Oran Mor); *In Time O' Strife*, *The Guid Sisters*, *Truant* (NTS); *Grit* (Pachamama); *Breaker* (Holden Street Adelaide); *Age of Arousal*, *The Cherry Orchard* (Lyceum Theatre); *That Face*, *Antigone* (Tron Theatre); *Washed up* (Oran Mor); *Sunset Song* (His Majesty's theatre); *The Last Witch* (Traverse Theatre); *The Ducky* (Borderline); *Romeo and Juliet* (Dundee Rep Theatre); *Yarn* (Grid Iron). Film/TV/radio credits include *Elf Factor*, *Badults*, *Case Histories*, *Rab C Nesbitt*, *Day of the Flowers*, *Storyville*, *Dis-Connected*, *Rebus*, *Mashed*, *Modrin McDonald*, *On Her Majesty's Service*, *I Remember Yesterday* and *Sunset Song*.

LEWIS HETHERINGTON

Lewis is a Glasgow-based Playwright and Performance Maker whose work is rooted in collaboration and story. As associate of Analogue he co-wrote *Mile End* and *Beachy Head,* and wrote the text of *2401 Objects.* With Catrin Evans he wrote and directed *Leaving Planet Earth* for Grid Iron at the Edinburgh International Festival. Other writing credits include *The Island, Khamsah* (National Youth Theatre); *The Fragmented Life of Dorothy Lawrence* (Royal Conservatoire of Scotland); *Instructions for Butterfly Collectors* (National Theatre of Scotland); *A Perfect Child* and *Sea Change* (Oran Mor). Work for young people includes *Friends Electric* (Visible Fictions); *Three Little Pigs, Red Riding Hood, Goldilocks* (Platform). His work with Ailie Cohen – *The Secret Life of Suitcases* (Unicorn) and *Cloud Man* – continues to tour extensively internationally. Lewis' work has been produced throughout the UK and internationally including performances in Australia, China, Saudi Arabia, Dubai, Germany, United States and Japan.

KANE HUSBANDS

Kane is a theatre director specialising in movement, physical theatre and choreography. He has his own Company 'The PappyShow', and is an associate for 'National Youth Theatre' and 'Squint Theatre'. Kane has just finished choreographing for National Youth Theatre's production of *The Merchant of Venice* in London's West End. Kane choreographed the Olympic and Paralympic Team Welcome Ceremonies and then went onto direct these for the 2014 Glasgow Commonwealth Games. Kane has choreographed dance-theatre pieces that have toured China, directed mass-ensemble site-specific performances and developed regional community theatre performances. His work has taken him across the UK, Europe and the Middle East. As a movement director, choreographer and facilitator, Kane has worked with National Theatre, Old Vic Theatre, MAC Birmingham, Sheffield Crucible, SCOOP Outdoor Theatre, Rose Bruford College, Royal Central School of Speech and Drama, National Youth Theatre, King Abdulaziz Centre for World Culture, National Theatre Scotland, Tricycle Theatre and others.

RHYS JARMAN

Rhys was one of the winners of the 2007 Linbury Biennial Prize, for his designs of Varjak Paw for the Opera Group. New work includes *The Wonderful Wizard of Oz* (Northern Stage); *The Time of Your Life* (Gecko and BBC co-production) and *Hurling Rubble at the Sun and Moon* (Park Theatre). Rhys has also designed Institute and Missing for Gecko and is currently working on 2 new shows for 1216 and 2017. Recent theatre work includes *The Nutcracker* with The Nuffield Theatre directed by Blanche McIntyre, *Holes* written by Tom Basden and *Threeway* written by DC Jackson both directed by Philip Breen. Outdoor work includes *Collective Endeavour*, *Burntwater* and *One Million* for Tangled Feet and The Greenwich and Docklands International Festival. Recent work for opera includes *Adriano in Syria* (The Classical Opera Company); *The Fairy Queen* (Temple Music Foundation); *Hot House* (Royal Opera House Education, main stage) and *The Barber of Seville* (ETO). Other works for theatre include *Diary of a Nobody* (Royal & Derngate Theatre); *Money The Game Show, Mission to Mars and The Moon, the Moon* (Unlimited Theatre); *Romeo and Juliet* (Night Light Theatre); *Time for the Good Looking Boy* and *A Christmas Carol* with Iqbal Khan. Designs for television include set designs for *Alice in Wonderland, Peter Pan* and *A Christmas Carol* for CBeebies, series 5 of *Dr Who* and *Young, Autistic and Stagestruck* for Channel 4. Twitter: @rhysjarman

DEVESH KISHORE

Stowaway marks Devesh's professional debut having recently graduated from Royal Welsh College of Music and Drama. Roles while training included Roderigo in *The Duchess of Malfi* directed by Greg Hersov; A in *Ring Ring* directed by Ned Bennett; Tartuffe in *Tartuffe* directed by Jamie Garven and Antonio in *The Merchant of Venice* directed by Simon Reeves.

HELEN MUGRIDGE

Helen is an experienced stage and production manager. Her previous credits include *Stowaway* (Analogue, National Tour); *Golem* (1927, UK and International tour); *Stand* (Chris Goode & Company, Oxford Playhouse); *Re-Enactments* (Analogue, Shoreditch Town Hall); *Mess* (Caroline Horton, National Tour); *The Secret Agent* (Theatre O, Edinburgh, Young Vic and National Tour); *The Victorian in the Wall* (Will Adamsdale, Royal Court and national tour); *Monkey Bars* (Chris Goode & Company, Edinburgh, tour and Unicorn); *Mass Observation* (Inspector Sands, Almeida Theatre); *Cooking Ghosts* (Beady Eye, South East tour and Camden People's Theatre); *Penumbra* (BYO, Thickskin – Research and development); *2401 Objects* (Analogue, National theatre and European development, Edinburgh 2011 and national and European tour); *The Adventures of Wound Man and Shirley* (Chris Goode & Company, Edinburgh 2011); *Total Football*, Ridiculusmus (Barbican Pit, Belfast Festival and Autumn 2012 tour); *Beachy Head* (Analogue, National and European Tour); *Everything Must Go* (Beady Eye/Kristin Fredrickson, National and European Tour).

PHILIP PINSKY

Philip Pinsky is a composer and sound designer. For five years he was Associate Artist at the Royal Lyceum, working on more than 25 productions. He has also provided scores for NTS, EIF, Chichester Festival Theatre, Traverse, Almeida, Dundee Rep, TNM (Montreal); Grid Iron, Stellar Quines, Lung Ha, Janis Claxton Dance, Magnetic North, Shetland Arts, Red Shift, Assembly, Imaginate, SCO, Sky Arts, MTV, Granada and BBC TV and Radio. Recent work includes; *The Crucible, Pressure* (Royal Lyceum); *Thingummy Bob* (Lung Ha/Luminate); *The Jennifer Tremblay Trilogy* (Stellar Quines); *Les Trois Mousquetaires, Cyrano De Bergerac* (TNM, Montreal); *The Driver's Seat* (NTS); *Blood Wedding* (Graeae/Dundee Rep/Derby Theatre) and *Letters Home* (Grid Iron/International Book Festival). Winner of the Critics Award for Theatre in Scotland 2005 and of a Sony Music Award for *Extraneous Noises Off* (BBC Radio 3). Previously he was founder member of electro-acoustic group Finitribe, releasing five albums and performing over a period of fifteen years.

STEVEN RAE

Steven trained at RSAMD. Recent theatre credits include *Cinderella* (Glasgow Life); *Scarfed For Life* (Citizens Theatre); *3 Little Pigs* (Platform); *Stowaway* (Analogue Theatre); *Slick, Dragon* (Vox Motus); *Princess For A Day* (Oran Mor); *Platypus in Boots* (Scottish Opera); *Little Ulla* (Citizens Theatre/Grinagaog); *Mr Snow* (Macrobert); *Aladdin* (Cumbernauld); *The Tempest*, *As You Like It*, *Hamlet*, *King Lear*, *Twelfth Night* (Bard In the Botanics); *Outspoken* (TAG); *Wee Fairy Tales*, *The Bevellers* (Citizens Theatre); *Passing Places*, *The Magistrate*, *The Flouers O' Edinburgh* (Pitlochry); *Snuff* (Arches/Traverse/NTS) and *Prince Unleashed* (Visible Fictions/BBC Scotland). Film/ TV credits include *Laid Off* (Incidental Pictures); *Princess For A Day* (Arnott Films); *Outpost, Rise of the Spetsnaz* (Black Camel Pictures); *Strayed* (Waugh Productions) and *The Last Laugh* (BBC Three).

IAN SMYTH

Ian is a Technical Stage Manager that has been trained in stage technologies, automation flying systems, counterweights flying and has a basic knowledge of performer flying and a good understanding of rigging and carpentry. Ian has recently graduated from the Royal Conservatoire of Scotland. His work varies in scale from large operas to small studio shows, including Sir John in *Love and Our House*, both at RCS. He also toured with All or Nothing Aerial Dance Theatre on their Three's a Crowd tour. Ian also teaches young people in America Technical Theatre.

BALVINDER SOPAL

Balvinder has worked with a number of award winning theatre companies nationally and internationally. Her career spans theatre, radio, film and television. Theatre credits include *Stowaway* (Analogue Theatre); *The Edge* (Transport Theatre); *Deranged Marriage* (Rifco Arts); *Home Sweet Home* (Freedom Studios); *The Snow Queen* (Trestle Theatre/International tour); *Our Glass House* (Common Wealth Co); *Behna* (Kali Theatre); *Tales of the Harrow Road* (Soho Theatre); *The House of Bilquis Bibi* (Tamasha/

Hampstead); *Counted?* (Look Left Look Right); *Mela* (WYPH). Radio credits include *Everyday Tales of Afghan Folk* (Radio 4 Series 1-4); *Granny Anne's Joke World* (Ceebeebies Series 1); *Brief Lives* (Radio 4); *The Wild Neighbour and the Willing Coward* (BBC World Service); *Enemy of the People* (Radio 4); *Silver Street* (2004-2010) regular character – Simran Kaur (BBC Asian Network). Film/ TV credits include *Coronation Street*, *Naachley London* (Avairy Films); *Honeycomb Lodge*, BATFA Award-Winning *White Girl* (BBC1); *Adha Cup* (Channel 4); *Waterloo Road* and *Emmerdale*.

MOLLY STOKER

Since leaving college in 2002, Molly has worked with a wide range of dance, opera and theatre companies, including Scottish Opera, Ballet Cymru and English Touring Opera. She spent four years in the technical department at Pitlochry Festival Theatre before going freelance in 2009. Her relights include opera – *Manon* (Scottish Opera, 2009); *Flavio* (English Touring Opera, 2011); ballet – *The Tempest* (Ballet Cymru, 2012); *A Midsummer Night's Dream* (2013); physical theatre – *The Thrill of it All* (Forced Entertainment, 2010); *Chelsea Hotel* (Earthfall, 2012); and drama – *Hamlet* (*Rapture Theatre Co., 2010*); *Nivelli's War* (*Cahoots* NI, 2014). She recently toured with English Touring Opera as Head of Lighting, relighting *Pelleas et Melisande* (2015) and *Tales of Hoffmann* (2015) on tour. She has also worked on Buxton Opera Festival every year since 2011.

RIC WATTS

Ric is Producer for Analogue, for whom he has produced all of the company's work including *Mile End, Beachy Head, 2401 Objects, Re-enactments, Transports*, and *Stowaway*. He is also Executive Producer for Unlimited Theatre (*The Giant & The Bear, MONEY the game show, The Noise, Play Dough* and *Am I Dead Yet?*); Producer and co-Founder of Chris Goode & Company (*Men in the Cities, Weaklings, STAND, Monkey Bars, GOD/ HEAD* and *The Adventures of Wound Man and Shirley*) and Executive Producer for the newly independent

Leeds-based international festival Transform. He also sits on the board of Cartoon de Salvo; on the advisory board for RashDash and the Large Grants committee at Wellcome Trust; as well as regularly mentoring emerging artists and producers in the North of England. Ric has previously produced for Cartoon de Salvo, Ridiculusmus, Kazuko Hohki, theimaginarybody, The TEAM, Filter and Schtanhaus, The Frequency D'ici, Laura Mugridge, Royal & Derngate, The Other Way Works, Slung Low, Queer Up North International Festival and Hannah Jane Walker and Chris Thorpe.

KATHARINE WILLIAMS

Katharine Williams is a lighting designer for live performance. She works in the UK and internationally. Her designs have been seen in China, Hong Kong, New Zealand, Canada, the USA, Mexico, Ireland, Holland, Spain, Italy, Germany, Armenia, Romania, Russia and the Czech Republic. As a filmmaker, she is currently collaborating with Clare Duffy on Extreme Light North. Katharine is lead artist on the *Love Letters to the Home Office* project which campaigns using art, words and theatre to stop the means-tested tiering of Human Rights that is currently in place in the UK for international families. She is the founder of the Crew for Calais initiative.

DIRECTOR'S NOTE

In 2010 we came across a tragic real-life story. A young man's frozen body was found in the car park of a DIY superstore in Richmond, South London. He had climbed into the wheel arch of a plane in the Middle East and his body was tipped out as the landing gear was lowered in its approach to Heathrow. This was not an isolated incident. There were many stories about equally desperate journeys from India, Africa, South and Central America. Some were about escape, others about running toward something seemingly better. All of them involved incredible risk.

Since then, the war in Syria has brought these stories into sharp focus. The image of the body of three-year-old Aylan Kurd washed up on a Turkish beach shocked the world, and the plight of over 4.6 million Syrian refugees has brought the debate much closer to home.

All of these stories made — and continue to make — a deep impression. It's impossible not to be moved by the extraordinary lengths these people go to in order to change their lives. But when it comes to making a show inspired by such stories, how could we, as white middle-class British citizens, possibly begin to understand and accurately portray something so deeply removed from our own experiences?

To help answer this, we took this extraordinary story to India. Our three week journey took us from Chennai to Kolkata, from national concert halls to rehearsal studios, community centres to school classrooms. Back in the UK, we met with refugees, asylum seekers, migrants from all over the world. Second or third generation Pakistanis, Indians, Africans, Syrians. Every meeting offered us a new interpretation of our story. We began to understand that there was no singular truth behind a story like this, but multiple voices, all overlapping and contradicting.

Throughout our making process, we've shared early versions of the show with the public, often to complex and conflicting responses. By and large, it is the Western, liberal, middle classes that have questioned our right to tell this man's story most, while the refugees and asylum seekers we have met have urged us on. These conversations have thrown up fascinating questions: What would it mean to not tell this story because it belongs to someone else? What is it about this particular story that feels so uncomfortable for us to tell? Can we only tell stories from our own direct experiences? And where are the lines we cannot cross?

Stowaway is our attempt to tell a version of this story, inspired by some remarkable real-life accounts. We hope it might open a door for some vital conversations about events that continue to unfold all around us today. Events that do not always happen far from home, and ones in which we may find ourselves playing a bigger part than we realise.

Hannah Barker and Lewis Hetherington

CREW FOR CALAIS

The team behind *Stowaway* are supporting the Crew for Calais initiative, which utitises the skills of individuals working in the theatre, event and production industries who have come together to build shelters for people in the Calais refugee camp.

The idea came from artist and theatre lighting designer, Katharine Williams, who visited the camp at Calais and wanted to help: "Most of the 7,000 refugees were still living in tents in December, despite the winter cold. One thing that theatre and event people are very good at, in my experience, is erecting wooden structures efficiently. I'm thinking of all those hundreds of get-ins we've done over the years. And so I came back to the UK with a plan."

There have already been a series of regional build sessions in London, Birmingham and Leeds, as well as trips to build with the charity A Home For Winter in Calais.

Companies and individuals in the industry wanting to donate time, talents and services, both in the UK and Calais can email CrewForCalais@gmail.com or volunteer via the Facebook group.

STOWAWAY

Hannah Barker & Lewis Hetherington

STOWAWAY

OBERON BOOKS
LONDON

WWW.OBERONBOOKS.COM

First published in 2016 by Oberon Books Ltd
521 Caledonian Road, London N7 9RH
Tel: +44 (0) 20 7607 3637 / Fax: +44 (0) 20 7607 3629
e-mail: info@oberonbooks.com
www.oberonbooks.com

A catalogue record for this book is available from the British Library.

PB ISBN: 9781783197477
E ISBN: 9781783197484

Cover design: Liam Jarvis

Printed, bound and converted
by CPI Group (UK) Ltd, Croydon, CR0 4YY.

Visit www.oberonbooks.com to read more about all our books and to buy them. You will also find features, author interviews and news of any author events, and you can sign up for e-newsletters so that you're always first to hear about our new releases.

Characters

ADITYA

DEBBIE

ANDY

LISA

SALMA

Additional Voices

HOST

PRESENTER

AGENT

CALL HANDLER

MAN

GUIDE

HEADTEACHER

PRESET

A diagonal line of chairs cuts across the space. A Plane. Passengers take their seats, settle in for a long flight.

Clearance. As lights fade down:

ANNOUNCEMENT:

This is your final call for flight BB787 to London Heathrow, please make your way to gate 37. This is your final call. Thank you.

Blackout.

'–' indicates when the person speaking is cut off by the next speaker

PROLOGUE

Lights up.

Passengers on a plane. They move from one position to another, shifting in slow motion. Suspended in placeless timeless flight. A score plays out below the entire action while we focus in and out of locations. A series of onboard flight announcements as part of the soundscape, standard announcements include:

ANNOUNCEMENT:

At this time we request that all mobile phones and electronic devices be turned off, for take off … cabin crew doors automatic cross check and report thank you … flight attendants prepare for take off … now we request your full attention as the flight attendants take you through the safety features onboard this aircraft … –

These announcements are cut short by various other audio excerpts crackling in as follows:

From Question Time.

— Why does India get all our foreign aid, when it's got several billion pounds to spend on its French fighter jets?

— The news of course today that the Indian government is negotiating a £6.3 billion contract for French fighters when –

From BBC Hindi (broadcast about David Cameron's visit to the site of the Amritsar Massacre).

>   … it's very mixed actually, somebody, a
>   few of them thanked Mr Cameron, and
>   a few of them are actually turning back
>   and saying, how does it really matter, this
>   happened years back and why should we
>   expect an apology, when nothing, we aren't
>   getting our people back, and how much
>   other episode of violence, within India,
>   perpetrated by Indians, how many times.

From Channel 4 News.

— Joining us now in the studio is Dr Maria Misra, a historian and an expert on India and the British Empire and Dabinderjit Singh, spokesperson for Sikh Federation United Kingdom. Dr Misra, should he have apologised?

— Yes. I think so. I mean I think it's about time the British did start apologising for their Empire. I think saying you feel remorse or that it was a shameful event is not enough –

From Passage to India.

— I'm longing to see something of the real India.

— Fielding, how is one to see the real India?

— Try seeing Indians!

— Who's that?

— Our Schoolmaster. Government College.

— As if one could avoid seeing them!

— Well I've scarcely spoken to an Indian since we landed.

— Lucky you!

The different images we see are as follows, this is a suggested order only.

1. Lisa has panic attack.
2. Andy nightmare.
3. Aditya on skyscraper.
4. Aditya and Salma on beach.
5. Lisa on scyscraper.
6. Debbie and Andy meeting headteacher.
7. Andy meets Lisa.
8. Salma tries to stop Aditya.
9. Aditya falling and floating.

PART ONE

1.

Book Festival event. LISA has just finished reading from her book. Sound of a plane landing.

HOST   Thanks so much for that reading from your book. It's not been without controversy this book has it?

LISA   I guess not.

HOST   What made you think you should tell this story? What really sparked it off?

LISA   Well it was sort of a surprise to me. I was planning to do the next one in the Greyforest series, that world I'd been in for some time, but then this thing happened to me, I was there, I couldn't just –

HOST   Let me rephrase the question, because of course we know that you were there, you were physically near when this tragic incident happened, but what gives you a connection to it? What made you think *you* could tell this story?

LISA   Sorry?

HOST   You're a privileged white woman, what made you think you were the one to tell it?

LISA   I er. I just thought I had to try. At least try and tell it.

2.

ANDY is holding two cups of coffee.

ANDY   Debbie? Debbie?

DEBBIE   You calling me?

ANDY   Yeah I was.

DEBBIE   I was just on my way out.

ANDY   I thought we could.

DEBBIE   You made coffee.

ANDY   Oh well.

DEBBIE   You did the foamy milk and everything.

ANDY   Yeah but.

DEBBIE   I can be late.

ANDY   Really?

DEBBIE   Yeah course. I've put in enough overtime
                lately.

ANDY   There you go.

DEBBIE   Thanks, that's really kind.

ANDY   Not like I have anything else to do.

DEBBIE   I keep saying, this is a chance to recharge.

ANDY   I want to be useful.

DEBBIE   You are.

ANDY   I want things to do.

DEBBIE   You could go to B&Q.

ANDY   Really?

DEBBIE   You love B&Q.

ANDY   I wouldn't say I love it.

DEBBIE   You've got a loyalty card.

ANDY   Yeah but.

11

DEBBIE	You could paint Sophie's room.
ANDY	Can we afford the paint?
DEBBIE	Andy you've only been redundant for three weeks. We can afford a tin of paint.

DEBBIE starts to get herself ready.

ANDY	She wants purple walls.
DEBBIE	Great.
ANDY	And a pink ceiling.
DEBBIE	If that's what she wants.
ANDY	Might cheer her up.
DEBBIE	Exactly.
ANDY	She won't talk about school now. At all.
DEBBIE	Can't get into this now Andy.
ANDY	Sorry.
DEBBIE	No it's fine it's just.
ANDY	She's got that new teacher maybe that'll be.
DEBBIE	It's not the teacher it's just. She just doesn't fit.
ANDY	Maybe I could do more with her.
DEBBIE	Yeah maybe.
ANDY	Like fishing or.
DEBBIE	Fishing? She's nine years old.
ANDY	Yeah maybe not fishing.
DEBBIE	Start with painting the bedroom.
ANDY	Yeah no you're right. Tell you what I'm going to do, I'm going to get cracking on

the house. Just 'til I get a new job. Do the gutters and –

DEBBIE   Yeah yeah that's a great idea. I do have to head off now. I'll be back late.

ANDY   They should pay you more.

DEBBIE   Well if the next few weeks go well. They will.

ANDY   Love you.

DEBBIE   Yes love you too. Oh and if you do go to B&Q just remember I need the car tonight.

ANDY   Yeah yeah course, on you go. I'll drink the coffees.

DEBBIE exits.

ANDY takes in the now quiet house. He turns on the radio. The words are spoken into an onstage microphone by one of the ensemble.

PRESENTER   And finally this morning India has announced plans to launch its first mission to mars. Chairman of the Indian Space Agency, Dr Radhakrishnan, says; 'India could become the first country in the world to reach Mars on its own steam in the first attempt.' Indeed the world will be watching as –

ANDY leaves. The radio is switched off.

3.

ANDY has been to B&Q. He is walking back to his car, on the phone.

ANDY   Hey Debbie. Got the paint. Hope everything's going well with all the big new clients and everything. Let me know what you want for dinner and I'll cook something nice. See you later.

What the …

He watches it fall. It falls and falls.

The body lands in front of ANDY.

Silence.

ANDY stares in horror.

He vomits.

He gets out his phone.

ANDY   Police.

I. I. I don't know what has happened.

There's a body. He's dead.

No. No. He's definitely … I saw him.

I'm fine I'm fine I just you need to.

He looks around.

It's just me.

Car park of B&Q.

The er … Upper Richmond Road.

OK. Yes. OK.

He stares at the body.

He eventually walks backwards.

4.

LISA is queuing to get off the plane. Talking to her agent on the phone.

ANNOUNCEMENT:

Please remain in your seats with your seatbelts fastened until we have opened the cabin doors.

LISA	I'm still on the plane. We're queuing to get off.
AGENT	Was the flight OK?
LISA	Boring. Fine.
AGENT	I got an email from the festival already.
LISA	Oh right.
AGENT	They were really happy with your event. It got lots of attention.
LISA	That's good.
AGENT	There's a big feature in the 'Gulf News'. It's a really important paper out there with a big online presence so it's got real reach.
LISA	Great.
AGENT	Did they look after you?
LISA	Oh yes. There was like twelve swimming pools and gold taps and everything.
AGENT	Wow.
LISA	Towels with my initials sown in. All that stuff.
AGENT	You're feeling a bit tired aren't you?
LISA	I've got a bit of a headache.
AGENT	Look we can talk later. I'll email over the new invitations and proposals.
LISA	Thanks.
AGENT	Go and get your luggage and get some sleep and we'll chat again soon.

5.

ANDY is at home. DEBBIE returns from work.

DEBBIE	Oh you're in here.
ANDY	Yeah.
DEBBIE	I didn't know if you were in.
ANDY	Yeah.
DEBBIE	Are you OK?
ANDY	Yes. Yeah. Yeah.
DEBBIE	How did it go with the painting?
ANDY	The what?
DEBBIE	Sophie's room?
ANDY	Oh shit I didn't –
DEBBIE	No worries. We can do it together at the weekend. All of us. Sophie can boss us about. It'll be fun.
ANDY	I just didn't even –
DEBBIE	It's not a big deal.
ANDY	I know it isn't.
DEBBIE	Right OK. I just have to dump some stuff here and head out again. Got to take those stands to the other office for tomorrow morning.
ANDY	Yeah.
DEBBIE	And I need that memory stick. The green one.
ANDY	Yeah.
DEBBIE	Have you seen it?

ANDY	What?
DEBBIE	Andy I don't have time for this.
ANDY	I'll help you with the stands what do you want me to –
DEBBIE	No there is obviously something wrong so just –
ANDY	There was a man in the car park at B&Q. He fell.

ADITYA begins to slowly move into a position reminiscent of how he landed in the car park.

DEBBIE	Oh.
ANDY	Yeah. It wasn't nice.
DEBBIE	What happened? Was he old or –
ANDY	What?
DEBBIE	Was he an old man?
ANDY	No. He wasn't.
DEBBIE	What happened?
ANDY	I don't know he fell and he was on the ground. There was all this blood and …
DEBBIE	Andy that's. Are you OK?
ANDY	I'm fine but.
DEBBIE	Was he alright?
ANDY	No.
DEBBIE	What did you do?
ANDY	Called 999. They took him away in an ambulance.
DEBBIE	Well that's good then.

ANDY	Yeah I'm.
DEBBIE	You did the right thing, you did what you could.
ANDY	I just. Can we talk about this later?

Just as he reaches the landing position, ADITYA unravels and disappears.

DEBBIE	Of course.
ANDY	You've got your thing to get to.
DEBBIE	Ok. If you're sure.
ANDY	Yes.
DEBBIE	Where did you park the car? Couldn't see it out front.
ANDY	It's not here.
DEBBIE	What?
ANDY	I left it at B&Q.
DEBBIE	Why?
ANDY	I just wanted to walk home.
DEBBIE	Along the dual carriageway?
ANDY	Get some peace.
DEBBIE	It's not exactly quiet.
ANDY	Yes I know I just didn't want to drive –
DEBBIE	I need the car.
ANDY	Yes well it's not here so.
DEBBIE	It'll take me an hour on the bus.
ANDY	Well I'm really sorry you're going to have to get the bus but I don't actually think it's that big a deal. Do you want me to run to

B&Q while you wait because if you really
want me to then –

DEBBIE exits while he is still talking.

6.

*LISA is at home, leafing through the newspaper, on the phone to her
AGENT.*

AGENT	There'll be another one straight after, at four.
LISA	Uh huh.
AGENT	Which is tight but I'll get you a cab.
LISA	Uh huh.
AGENT	It'll be on account. And it'll have the address already
LISA	Right.
AGENT	so you don't need to worry about that.
LISA	Right.
AGENT	And then they've got a little conference room so you can do the interview from there.
LISA	Great.
AGENT	They'll talk you through it all on the day.

LISA has noticed something.

LISA	…
AGENT	Will that be OK? The guy there Mark is great and he'll speak to you.
LISA	…
AGENT	Lisa?

LISA	I just. What time did I land last week?
AGENT	What?
LISA	When I flew in from Dubai last week. What time did my flight get into Heathrow? Roughly?
AGENT	Er. I can actually probably find it … yep here we go. Nine fifteen.
LISA	God.
AGENT	What is it?
LISA	There's this story in the paper. About a man on that plane.

ADITYA is in the wheelarch freezing to death.

	He had hidden in the wheels somehow and he froze to death. And then his body fell out.
AGENT	Oh god. What happened?
LISA	It landed in a car park. When they put the wheels down for landing it, the body, he fell out. I was on that plane.
AGENT	That's awful.
LISA	Yes …
AGENT	Do you want me to come over?

ADITYA unravels from his position and disappears.

LISA	No.
AGENT	I can cancel these interviews this afternoon.
LISA	God no. No don't do that. Sorry I've not been paying any attention. Sorry.
AGENT	Do you want to call me back in a bit?

LISA   No. No it's totally fine.

She puts the newspaper aside.

                         I'm all yours. But probably best to start
                         from the beginning.

7.

ANDY is on the line to the Police, dealing with a Call Handler on a switchboard.

ANDY   Yeah. It was a few days ago. I was in the
                         B&Q car park –

CH   Right OK well if you could give me the
                         name please?

ANDY   Andrew Fielding.

CH   Ok I'll see if I can find him.

ANDY   No. I'm Andrew Fielding.

CH   Right well I will need the name of the
                         person you want to speak to.

ANDY   I don't know the name of the person.

CH   Ok.

ANDY   Last week. There was a man. In the B&Q
                         car park. He fell.

CH   And what was your involvement? Was your
                         car damaged or.

ANDY   No I was a witness.

CH   Ok you were a witness to a crime –

ANDY   No I was a witness to, a body falling.

CH   You saw an accident?

ANDY	I spoke to the officer who told me to call this number.
CH	Right, was the man violent, or under the influence of alcohol.
ANDY	No he wasn't drunk what are –
CH	I'm just trying to best place your call –
ANDY	He was dead. His body was exploded all over the car park. That's what I saw.
CH	Are you looking to make an application to the criminal injuries compensation scheme?
ANDY	What? You're asking me if –
CH	I'm really sorry sir. But I just want to know how to best place your call.
ANDY	I spoke to an officer. I was told to call this number if I had any – I just want to know what happened to him.
CH	And what is your connection to the –
ANDY	There is no connection I just saw him. It. I –
CH	Ok Sir. I'm going to do my best to –
ANDY	Just forget it. It's fine.
CH	If you have new information it is important that –
ANDY	No no. It doesn't matter. I really don't have anything to do with this at all I … Thanks.

He hangs up.

He puts the phone aside.

The phone rings.

After a time he answers.

LISA	Hello. Is this Andrew Fielding?
ANDY	Yes.
LISA	My name is Lisa Cohen. I understand you were involved in an incident recently.
ANDY	I am not interested in talking to the papers. I don't know how you got this number but –
LISA	I'm not a reporter.
ANDY	I don't believe you so –
LISA	I was on the plane.
ANDY	What plane?
LISA	The one he was on.
ANDY	What?
LISA	He was beneath my feet.
ANDY	Is this a joke?
LISA	I wanted to talk to you.
ANDY	Well I'm sorry but I'm not. I'm really not interested.
LISA	But perhaps if …
ANDY	You're wasting your time.

ANDY hangs up on LISA.

He switches on TV. The words are spoken into an onstage microphone by one of the ensemble.

—	I don't think delusion is too strong a word, for a country like India to be building a space programme when 400 million people still live without electricity, 600 million people live without a toilet.

23

—   Ok but if we look at the statistics, this
            mission actually only cost about four rupees
            per person in India. That's not even four
            pence. And if you're suggesting a country
            shouldn't have a space programme if they
            have issues with poverty then no nation in
            the world could continue to undertake this
            kind of research.

*ADITYA pulls on a final layer of clothes. He sneaks his way through
a hole in the fence, and makes his way across the airfield. He climbs
the tyre and metal leg into the wheelarch.*

8.

*DEBBIE and ANDY's house. ANDY has fallen asleep in front of TV.
ADITYA is in the wheelarch as the plane begins to gather pace. Louder
and louder until ANDY wakes from a nightmare with a start. DEBBIE
enters, she has been working.*

*LISA is at home on her laptop/iPad. Throughout the scene, she reads
phrases aloud as she types them and clicks to search.*

DEBBIE	Andy? Are you OK?
ANDY	Yeah. Yeah I just. Bad dream.
DEBBIE	What was it?
LISA	Immigrant Dubai Plane.
ANDY	Nothing. Didn't mean to disturb you.
DEBBIE	Don't be silly.
ANDY	You're working.
DEBBIE	It's fine.
ANDY	My head's buzzing.
DEBBIE	You shouldn't sleep in front of the TV.
ANDY	Was that? Is that a noise?

DEBBIE	Don't think so.
ANDY	Do you think I woke Sophie?

DEBBIE listens.

DEBBIE	No no you won't have.
ANDY	Debbie. That man I saw fall in the car park.
DEBBIE	The other week?
ANDY	Yes.

LISA typing.

LISA	Stowaway found Richmond.

She clicks and scrolls through results.

ANDY	It was a dead man. He fell out of a plane that was coming into land at Heathrow.
DEBBIE	My god. How did he fall out?
ANDY	He was hidden in the wheel arch.

LISA typing.

LISA	Asylum seeker Plane Wheel Arch.

She clicks and scrolls through results.

DEBBIE	Oh how awful.
ANDY	Yeah.
DEBBIE	And you found the body?
ANDY	Yeah. It was. I should have told you.
DEBBIE	It's OK.
ANDY	I didn't know how to say it and I didn't want another thing on your plate, and I thought it would just go away but I keep thinking about it. Him.

DEBBIE   Well yeah of course you would.

ANDY   It was horrible.

DEBBIE   Oh Andy.

ANDY   There was all this stuff round his head and
              I didn't know if it was vomit or his brains
              or. It was unreal.

DEBBIE   I'm so sorry.

ANDY   Why would someone do that? Get into the
              underbelly of a plane? What could possibly
              make you –

DEBBIE   Well it's, it's impossible to get your head
              round isn't it?

LISA   Man falls from Dubai plane.

ANDY   He died mid-flight. He was dead for hours
              when I found him.

LISA typing.

She clicks and scrolls through results.

ANDY   But still I think of him. I see him. I keep
              seeing him everywhere.

DEBBIE   Right well, it'll take time but you'll get over
              it.

ANDY   Get over it?

DEBBIE   Not like. I mean it'll fade and you'll start to
              feel normal again.

ANDY   I'm not going to just get over it. I saw him
              fall out the sky.

DEBBIE   I know. I know. It's just. Horrible things
              happen in the world and, this is one of

those awful horrible things. But you can't,
you can't let it all in. You'd go crazy.

I'm really sorry, Andy, I should have asked
I should've known something was –

ANDY	You've been busy.
DEBBIE	Yes but –
ANDY	It's fine. You can get back to your work.
DEBBIE	I'm pretty much done. Might just go to bed. You want to come up or …
ANDY	You go on. I might watch something rubbish on the telly. My brain's awake.

LISA has found some pictures, she clicks through them. Reacts.

ANDY watches TV. The words are spoken into an onstage microphone by one of the ensemble. ADITYA appears next to him upon the skyscraper.

| — | It's about ambition, about India getting a seat at the world table with the big boys, and I don't think that's a bad thing. It's about pushing education, industry, technology but also it's about hope, ambition, and you know this is outer space, its the frontier. You don't want to be left behind. |

9.

LISA and ANDY in cafe.

ANDY	Sorry I hung up on you last week.
LISA	That's OK. I'm glad you phoned back. Do you live near here?
ANDY	Around the corner.

LISA	Right.
ANDY	Take you long to get here?
LISA	Not really. It's nice.
ANDY	Yeah. I come here quite a bit. Since I lost my job.
LISA	Oh. Well I'm a writer so I spend half my life in cafes.
ANDY	Yeah you said on the phone. That's exciting.
LISA	I like it.
ANDY	Anything I'd know?
LISA	I don't know. They're crime novels. The Greyforest series.
ANDY	With the autistic pensioner detective?
LISA	Well I don't call him that but –
ANDY	They're everywhere.
LISA	Well.
ANDY	That's amazing.
LISA	No it's really nothing it's … I brought that article.

LISA gets it out and hands it to him.

ANDY	I didn't see this one.
LISA	Yes I brought it because it's the only one that goes into any detail.

He reads.

ANDY	But it's. It's not right.
LISA	Really?

ANDY	Well it says he was found at nine forty-five which is wrong. I found him at like quarter past.
LISA	What about the rest of it?
ANDY	He had a tiny piece of like thread round his wrist. Like goldy yellowy. They've missed that. And he had like a dark blue jumper thing. Not red.
LISA	Oh.
ANDY	And it wasn't plain. There was this, like a … company logo or something on it. Sort of skyscrapers, a cityscape.
LISA	Really? Makes you wonder what else is wrong.
ANDY	I know.
LISA	Didn't the press want to speak to you?
ANDY	They tried. The BBC. Loads of the free papers. A Swedish TV channel.
LISA	But you didn't –
ANDY	No. I was. I didn't think I had anything to say. But now, looking at this, I mean this guy they've spoken to, he didn't turn up til after the Police arrived. I remember his little face peering over the police tape trying to get a good look. Wanting to see the body.
LISA	Someone took a picture.
ANDY	What?
LISA	I found it online when I was doing some research. Just on their phone, they took a

picture of his face as he lay there in the car park and they just stuck it up online. It's horrible.

ANDY   People are awful.

LISA   Pretty much. *(Reacting to the sound of a plane overhead.)* That's really loud.

ANDY   Yeah, we're in the flight path so.

LISA   Sounds like they're right above your head.

ANDY   We've lived here for ages so I'm used to it. Well I was. Now, every time I hear them I.

LISA   I know.

Pause.

Phone rings.

ANDY   Oh sorry, I should just.

LISA   Of course.

ANDY   Hi.

DEBBIE   Andy, I just popped back, but you weren't.

ANDY   No, I nipped out for a bit.

DEBBIE   Where are you?

ANDY   Just in a café.

DEBBIE   Oh right.

ANDY   Everything OK?

DEBBIE   You left the back door open.

ANDY   Did I?

DEBBIE   Yeah. And all the breakfast things are still.

ANDY   Yeah, I was planning to get to them when I got back.

DEBBIE	And Sophie's room? Are you still going to.
ANDY	Can we talk about this later?
DEBBIE	Yes. Yes OK.
ANDY	Ok then.
DEBBIE	I should be back about –
ANDY	Yep fine. Bye.
DEBBIE	Bye.
ANDY	*(Indicating to phone.)* My wife.
	She's being really patient but I don't think she. She doesn't understand. It's not her fault, she couldn't possibly …
LISA	I know.
ANDY	I thought by now I would've felt.
LISA	Me too.
ANDY	But he's.
LISA	Everywhere.
ANDY	Exactly. Are you going to write about this?
LISA	Well I don't know. I spoke to a few blogs about doing a little response piece on irregular migration. Maybe tying in something about the way words migrate across languages and cultures.
ANDY	Right. That sounds interesting. Do you do much of that stuff, bloggy stuff?
LISA	Not really.
ANDY	I mean I just know your books.

LISA	I know I just thought with this I should do something different. I don't really have any connection to him.
ANDY	But you were on the plane with him. You were there when he died.

Fleeting moment of LISA on her journey home from Dubai. She has a moment of anxiety.

10.

ANDY and LISA at his house. They have been there for some time.

LISA	And so all this time, his body is just what, sitting in a freezer somewhere?
ANDY	Yeah 'cos see the Home Office want to send it to Dubai because that's where the plane came from.
LISA	But the Dubai authorities won't allow it?
ANDY	No because they are saying he is Indian so the body should go there.
LISA	How did you find all that out?
ANDY	I've called the police, quite a few times. Took ages but I got through to the officer I met in the car park. He told me.
LISA	And what are they going to do now?
ANDY	It's out of their hands I think. I'm not sure he was really meant to tell me what he did to be honest.
LISA	Hey look I found this. Does this look like the logo that was on his clothes?
ANDY	I think so. Yes. Maybe.

LISA	It's a company called 'Skyline'. It looks like a construction company or.
ANDY	OK.
LISA	I mean it might not mean anything.
ANDY	But it looked like a uniform. It must mean something.
	Send the logo to print. We should start building up like a file.
LISA	Ok how do I.
ANDY	It's wireless.
LISA	Right where do I.
ANDY	It's that one. Click on that.
LISA	Ah OK that's it sent to print. So this company, do you think they're based in Dubai?
ANDY	Maybe. Or somewhere else in the Middle East. Or the rest of the world.
LISA	We might be here for some time.
ANDY	I could open a bottle of wine.
LISA	Well, I mean if you're –

DEBBIE enters.

ANDY	Debbie. You're home.
DEBBIE	Why weren't you answering your phone?
ANDY	It's upstairs I think. Sorry. This is Lisa who –
DEBBIE	Andy. I've called you like twenty times I didn't know what the hell was going on –
ANDY	Well I'm fine. Sorry but –

DEBBIE	You left Sophie at school. She was on her own for two hours.
ANDY	Fuck.
DEBBIE	The head called my office. They had to pull me out of a meeting. He found her hiding in the bike shed.
ANDY	Is she OK?
DEBBIE	Nothing happened if that's what you mean but –
ANDY	She must have been so upset she –
DEBBIE	It's no use caring now –
ANDY	Come on –
DEBBIE	What the hell were you thinking?
LISA	I think I should –
ANDY	You don't have to –
DEBBIE	Really Andy?
ANDY	Look, let's just
DEBBIE	What?
ANDY	I was going to get a bottle of wine, maybe we should have.
DEBBIE	Are you being funny?
LISA	I really think I should –
DEBBIE	I think that might be –
ANDY	No Lisa you don't have to –
DEBBIE	Andy you left our daughter at school what were you –
ANDY	We were researching into the stowaway –

DEBBIE   What?

ANDY   We were making progress.

DEBBIE   I don't care.

ANDY   You don't care about this man's life you –

DEBBIE   I don't give a fuck about this man and your
                stupid fucking project. Little Scooby gang
                trying to solve the mystery.

ANDY   That's what you think?

LISA gathers her things.

DEBBIE   What are you hoping to achieve –

ANDY   Lisa please one minute.

LISA   I'm going to –

DEBBIE   – what progress did you make that was
                worth this?

LISA exits.

                Seriously Andy where is your head?

*ANDY late at night, watching TV. ADITYA appears sitting next to
him. He is on the bus on his way to Dubai.*

*Panel discussion. The words are spoken into an onstage microphone
by one of the ensemble.*

—   To be honest I'm amazed that so many
                British people still seem to hold the colonial
                mindset that we should be telling the Indian
                people whether they should have a space
                programme or not. Given the absolutely
                horrific legacy of the British Empire in India.

—   Now I don't know what we gain from
                reaching back into history.

—   It might make us apologise.

	No look I. I'm simply saying that Health care, sanitation is more important than what you described as 'getting a seat at the world table'.
—	You fail to understand the significance of India's status on the global platform because where you come from you don't have to fight for an invitation.

11.

ANDY	Sorry about last week.
LISA	It's fine. Is everything OK with …
ANDY	Yes. Absolutely. I think with my redundancy and then all this. Left me a bit all over the place.
LISA	Of course. I think it's the same for me. Travelling everywhere to do press stuff for the book left me just, feeling a bit lost.
ANDY	I never would let this get to me normally.
LISA	Exactly and that's why it feels so important.
ANDY	What?
LISA	That we had our eyes open to this.
ANDY	Lisa. I don't know what I thought I was doing but –
LISA	Like you said in that cafe we are dealing with the fact that we were there –
ANDY	Look. Really. This whole thing has nothing to do with me.
LISA	You found his body.
ANDY	Yeah but.

LISA	It landed in front of you.
ANDY	So it was some sort of magical omen?
LISA	No but.
ANDY	I'm just done with this hanging over me.
LISA	So am I. That's why we have to do something about it.
ANDY	What are we going to do? What is the plan?
LISA	Write the book. About him. You said –
ANDY	Then write it. Do whatever you want. Leave me out of it.
LISA	But it's not the first time this happened. It's going to keep happening. I found out there have been 103 attempts since 1947,
ANDY	Exactly. It's just a thing that happens.
LISA	But that's just the ones that were recorded, what about the bodies which are never found, or ignored, or fall into the sea. Who knows what happened to them, what they –
ANDY	Exactly who knows?
LISA	We were doing this together.
ANDY	What are we doing?
LISA	I thought. I came over to say I thought we could go to India.
ANDY	Why?
LISA	To see if we can track down the family. Or I don't know. I thought we could volunteer we could. I haven't really thought about.
ANDY	I'm just to magic up a grand for plane tickets so we can wander round India?

LISA	It's actually only about eight hundred pounds.
ANDY	Only eight hundred? Great no problem!
LISA	What if I paid?
ANDY	Don't waste your money buying me a plane ticket to India. Buy yourself something. Or hey even better give it to charity, if you feel bad somehow because you got paid loads of money to go to a book festival in Dubai and flew home business class whilst a man died centimetres under your feet then take the eight hundred quid out the bank and go and give it to a charity. Give it to a beggar on the street. Or I don't know, put yourself in a helicopter and fly over Tower Hamlets and throw the money down on the poor people below.
LISA	You're being an idiot.
ANDY	No I'm being normal. You're not going to solve this. Stop trying to. Shit things happen and a bit of cash and sympathy from you is not going to make it all better.
LISA	That is not what I'm trying to.
ANDY	I'm out. Lisa. I'm done.

ANDY leaves.

DEBBIE enters.

DEBBIE	Hi. Sorry about that. At least one of us always trying to throw you out. He doesn't mean to get worked up. He's all over the place. And I'm sorry that I lost my temper that other time. But when you have a family

	you'll understand, you have to look after your own. What are you going to do now?
LISA	I'm going to write a book. About this.
DEBBIE	Oh. Right.
LISA	You meant as in, now this moment.
DEBBIE	Well.
LISA	That's embarrassing.
DEBBIE	No no it isn't, shall I call a cab or.
LISA	No it's fine. I'll be on my way.
DEBBIE	Lisa, just to say. I think it's great what you're doing. It's important that people are passionate. And doing stuff for charity and. I'm rambling but you know what I mean.
LISA	Thank you.
DEBBIE	It's really good of you to do things, for the greater good.
LISA	I don't know if I am. I'm just trying to make sense of it for myself if anything.

ADITYA is present.

PART TWO

12.

ADITYA	I am in the wheel arch of a plane. Contorted around rivets and bolts.
	The plane starts to move, and then begins tearing along the runway. My body rattles and jolts as the plane lifts off the ground.
	The engines are a wall of sound pushing against me. I am swallowed by a heavy cloud of heat. It is hot. The sound fills my ears.
	The wheels fold in but there is a thin line of light creeping through, golden light on my wrist. I can hear a voice. I'm five years old. I'm on the beach. I can hear my sister's voice.
SALMA	Adhi? Adhi?
ADITYA	Haan?
SALMA	Aap ko pata hai, boats Kahan jati hain? Right at the edge where the water ends?
ADITYA	What?
SALMA	They get smaller and smaller and then, they're gone!
ADITYA	And we're eight years old. Picking up bits of metal we find on the beach and she says –
SALMA	How will you be able to afford a plane?
ADITYA	Everyone will have them by then. We'll all have like mini planes or hoverboards or something. It'll just be normal. Zooming about with a jetpack. When we're old flying'll just be like normal.

SALMA	You're so stupid.
ADITYA	And I'm fourteen.
SALMA	Hum yahan rahengai. When we move out of our home … Right in front of the beach. When we're older we should get one of the big houses down here. Then we could just walk across the road and be at the sea. All of us.
ADITYA	And I'm eighteen.

13.

SALMA	Yeah he's OK. And yes he was more … professional than I thought.
ADITYA	There you go.
SALMA	Yes. I was wrong.
ADITYA	Uske paas Mercedes hai, man!
SALMA	I noticed.
ADITYA	And he sorts everything. Travel to Dubai. Visa. Accommodation. Forms. I just have to work. And maybe get myself a nice car.
SALMA	You can't even drive.
ADITYA	Come on. He sends hundreds of workers out there. He has contacts. He sets people up. That's how he made his paisa.
SALMA	It's all about the money with you.
ADITYA	No.
SALMA	Haan. Humesha paisey ki baatyn karty ho.
ADITYA	No.
SALMA	You can make money here you know.

ADITYA	I'm not just doing this for the money.
SALMA	That's not what you told Mum and Dad.
ADITYA	I know yes, I told them that because money makes sense to them. But you know me better. I want you to understand. I don't want you to be unhappy for me to go.
SALMA	But you'd be unhappy to stay and then that'd be my fault.
ADITYA	Come on.
SALMA	Look I understand. It's amazing. You can go and work on your skyscrapers and have a hundred wives in a hundred sports cars. And your agent person –
ADITYA	Recruiter.
SALMA	Yeah you know he seems very impressive. But don't get caught up in this. You can get work here.
ADITYA	I know.
SALMA	Well. Think about both options.
ADITYA	I'm a no one here.
SALMA	You're not a no one.
ADITYA	No I mean I'm just any one. Just one of hundreds of thousands of people who are all the same. Piled on top of each other and doing nothing.
SALMA	Like me?
ADTIYA	You have things here. You're getting married.
SALMA	And that's it for me?

ADITYA	You want to be here. You have a job. I spend my life on this beach, the city there, the sea there, and all these people just staring out to the horizon. I just want to … I want to be above it all.
SALMA	You could do that here.
ADTIYA	No.
SALMA	People are coming here now Adhi. To work.
ADITYA	Yeah right.
SALMA	From all over the world.
ADITYA	Yeah they come and stay in hotels and leave again.
SALMA	No. People who live here, they have companies unky paas companies hain.
ADITYA	Kaun?
SALMA	Dina's cousin has an internet start-up.
ADITYA	Dina's cousin does not have an internet start-up.
SALMA	He's always shutting himself away with his laptop.
ADITYA	There is only one reason he shuts himself away with his laptop.
SALMA	Addy that is disgusting.
ADITYA	That's the modern hyper connected India Salma!
SALMA	Oh be quiet. You're like a little boy.
ADITYA	…
SALMA	Will you come back?

ADITYA	Is that what this is about?
SALMA	Because you'll always be here anyway.
ADITYA	What does that mean?
SALMA	Just you will. This place is part of you. And you're part of this place.
ADITYA	Yeah fine I get that but I'm also going to be part of something bigger elsewhere, Dubai, America, China, the whole word is there and I want to see it.
SALMA	I don't think I could stop you if I tried.
ADITYA	So you'll talk to Mum and Dad. Persuade them?
SALMA	I'll talk to them.
ADITYA	And she does. She says to him.
SALMA	Dad, you left your village to see the city, and now it's Aditya's turn. He is leaving the city to see the world.
ADITYA	You said that to Dad?
SALMA	Yeah I told him. There's no gaps anymore. The world is getting smaller. You go where the money is.
ADITYA	Thank you Salma. Thank you thank you thank you. You're brilliant.
SALMA	Yes yes you don't need to thank me.

She picks something up off the beach. A golden thread.

ADITYA	Ok.
SALMA	No actually you do. But you can thank me with I don't know, a house with a

	swimming pool on the roof. When you come back home as the big man.
ADITYA	No problem.
SALMA	No actually you can thank me by not doing something stupid.
ADITYA	That might be a little bit more difficult.
SALMA	…
ADITYA	What's that?
SALMA	Don't know. A piece of dhaga.
ADITYA	It's nice.
SALMA	Hold your hand out.

He does so. She ties it round his wrist.

ADITYA	I will build you that house. When I come back here. I'll build a house right here. And one for Mum and Dad. They'll be nice. Modern. Stylish. And we can look out to sea whenever we want and to buy mango for breakfast every morning.
SALMA	That sounds nice.
ADITYA	And it's the day I'm leaving. We are walking to the Bus but I come down to the sea and –
SALMA	Adhi, Adhi aap Kya kar rahye ho?
ADITYA	Nothing.
SALMA	We've got to get to –
ADITYA	I know I'm just.
SALMA	What?
ADITYA	Nervous.

SALMA	You'll be fine.
ADITYA	Hope so.
SALMA	Course you will.
ADITYA	I didn't know you could see into the future.
SALMA	Stop messing about.
ADITYA	Alright, alright am I not allowed to –
SALMA	What?
ADITYA	Just be a bit unsure, don't know how this will –
SALMA	We've given everything to this Adhi. Dad sold the shop for this.
ADITYA	OK OK. I just –
SALMA	Just nothing Addy. This is what you wanted. You're getting the responsibility you always asked for. Right?
ADITYA	Yes. Good.
SALMA	You told us this was a sure thing. That's why I.
ADITYA	It is a sure thing. I'm not. It's little butterflies. Main soch raha hoon, khana kesa hoga. Mera boss kesa hoga. Little things.
SALMA	Adhi, humyen aap par proud hai.
ADITYA	I know. You'll barely notice I'm gone.
SALMA	…
ADITYA	It's OK. Come on you'll make me miss my bus.

14.

Going to Dubai.

ADITYA	And I'm on the bus. It pulls through the thick heat of the desert and winds round a corner and the city emerges. Great towers of glass and metal erupt from the sand, glistening. Buildings which cut out the ground and into the sky, leaving the dull earth below.
	The window melts and I float towards the city. A monster inviting me to dance.
—	This way please.
ADITYA	A line of shuffling men. Other buses are arriving. We're far outside the city. Low level ugly buildings.
—	You need to give me your passport.
ADITYA	Sorry?
—	Just your passport please, we need to make sure your Visa is processed and you can start to work.
ADITYA	Ok.

Hands over his passport.

—	This way please I'll take you to where you'll stay.
ADITYA	I think I need to wait for my passport.
—	No.
ADITYA	I just gave it to the man there and –
—	What? Are you going on holiday?
ADITYA	No.

—	Then what's the problem?
ADITYA	There isn't one I just.
—	Everyone gives in their passports. That's the way it works to get everything processed properly, so you need to move on now. If you have questions you can ask me later.
ADITYA	I arrive at a tiny hut. A stream of something runs outside the door. Glistening and thick. I step in it. It is sewage. We all walk in the hut and stand there. Embarrassed. There are six bunk beds but eight of us are told –
—	This is where you'll sleep.
ADITYA	Where is the man who was at that desk?
—	He's busy.
ADITYA	He said if I had any questions I could ask him …

The door shuts.

ADITYA	But he's gone. And there I am. A windowless room. And night falls sharp as a pin. Light but with devastating precision. There is the low hum of a generator. It's thick with heat. I can't sleep. I can feel myself rising and rising and it's so cramped in this tiny hut and I think –

Phone call.

SALMA	Adhi?
ADITYA	Salma?
SALMA	Aur Kaun? You've only just left and you've forgotten me. Too busy driving around in fast cars to remember your sister.
ADITYA	Yeah that's right.

SALMA	So what is it like?
ADITYA	How's Mum and Dad?
SALMA	Ammi papa, sub theek hai. Apart from they want to know how you are. What's –
ADITYA	And are you OK?
SALMA	I'm fine.
ADITYA	And what about –
SALMA	Haan Haan. Sub kuch theek hai. Sub vaisa ke vaisa hai. Tide rolls in and out. Markets go up and down. People look out to sea. I want to hear about you. I know you've only just arrived but …
ADITYA	…
SALMA	Adhi?
ADITYA	Salma I –
SALMA	Are there women there? Do you, like, get to go out and … see, Dina thinks you're going to meet some beautiful blond girl but how –
ADITYA	Salma, I don't know if –
SALMA	Actually don't tell me, I don't think I want to know.
ADITYA	I think. I think I've.
SALMA	What's your accommodation like?
ADITYA	Small.
SALMA	Sach mey?
ADITYA	There's quite a few of us sharing.

49

SALMA	Well did you see the city yet? Vo Kya kahtey hain … The Skygrazer Aur vo The Diamond Tower? I showed that picture of Dubai to Mum.
ADITYA	Really?
SALMA	– She put it up on the wall in the kitchen.
ADITYA	…
SALMA	Adhi you still there?
ADITYA	Yeah.
SALMA	Sub kuch theek to hai, nah?
ADITYA	I'm good. It's great … There's so many possibilities here. I think I want to try and get a promotion.
SALMA	You've only just got there!
ADITYA	I know but there are these guys with clipboards. And they're in charge. Guys like me, not all white guys you know? They noticed me, they think I'm funny. I'm going to work hard and get a job like that.
SALMA	Wow, so it really is …
ADITYA	Yeah. It's beautiful, Sal. We're right outside the city but I can see the lights.
SALMA	Really?
ADITYA	So many lights. On the far horizon a line of twinkling light.
SALMA	Why do you have to be so mystical all the time, Adhi?
ADITYA	Because I am here where it happens. In the warm glow. I've got to go.

15.

LISA in hotel room.

—	Hello Madam I'll take your luggage.
LISA	It's fine.
—	Please.
LISA	I'm fine.
—	If you'd follow me to the welcome desk?
LISA	Thanks.

LISA is at the check-in desk.

—	Ah it says you stayed here with us last month. Is that right?
LISA	Yes. For the book festival.
—	I'll just need your passport.
LISA	Of course.
—	Are you here for work again?
LISA	Sort of.
—	Well, we are very pleased to have you back and I hope we can be of service to you in any way you need.
LISA	Thank you.

LISA is handed her passport.

—	Let me help you with your bags.
LISA	No no I.

LISA is in her room.

LISA	Yes, yes this is all fine.

51

—	And if you change your mind about the spa treatments do let us know.
LISA	I won't, I don't want.
—	Very good. May I help you with anything else?
LISA	Well. What is the. I want to see Dubai. You know get a real sense of how it works. Get under the skin.
—	We can arrange a tour, a personal driver would take you to some of the beautiful buildings and a very authentic market experience and if you're interested there are a number of galleries which –
LISA	Right. I'll. Thank you for your help.

She sits down on her bed. Stares out the window. She wonders what she is doing.

ADITYA is present.

She sees a plane, so does ADITYA. They watch it across the sky.

16.

ADITYA	I'm at work. I've been here for weeks.
	The days slip by. We are in service to the skyscraper. Spine of steel and scales of concrete. I still haven't been paid. The air is thick with money which swarms and rushes into certain hands. But not mine. There must be a trick, some corner of the air to reach your hand in. But I'm. I'm just working. I still can't sleep at night but I'll work hard and get noticed. It is just so hot and the sound of the engines, the plane is still climbing the sound swallows me up and –

Phone call.

SALMA	Congratulations
ADITYA	Yeah well.
SALMA	Supervisor eh?
ADITYA	Yeah that's it.
SALMA	That's amazing Adhi.
ADITYA	Yes it is.
SALMA	Aur paisa? They'll pay you more money right?
ADITYA	Yes, of course.
SALMA	And when …
ADITYA	When what?
SALMA	When will … Sorry Adhi, I'm so proud of you, you're doing so well. I just wondered when you might be able to send us. It's just Dad is, well he's not doing.. and we're …
ADITYA	Don't worry, Salma. It's coming. It really is. There's all these processes. It's the way things have to be done here to. Boring administrative stuff. Paperwork and … but it won't be long and then I'll send money, I promise. Really soon. I've got to go.
SALMA	Really?
ADITYA	Yeah I've got to go.
—	You have to pay the money for your visa.
ADITYA	I thought I paid that.
—	This is for the validation and checking service.

ADITYA   When do I get paid?

—   You've only been here three weeks. You get
                your money at the end of the month.

ADITYA   And I do. I am paid one hundred and
                sixty two dollars. My recruitment fee was
                one thousand, six hundred and sixty-two
                dollars.

                I begin to build my own desert of hours,
                one grain at a time.

                We work fourteen-hour days. After a month
                of not sleeping things change and I just
                black out. Doesn't feel peaceful but at least
                it blocks out the noise, the heat and the
                streams of shit outside the hut. I black it
                all out and sleep. And wake up and work.
                Black out wake up. I move between sleep
                and the noise of it all. I can do this.

                I'm on my way. I can do this.

            Sound of construction site and plane engines.

—   You've got to work again tonight.

ADITYA   I've just come off shift.

—   You need to cover Ahmed.

ADITYA   What happened to Ahmed?

—   He fell.

ADITYA   Is he alright?

—   No.

ADITYA   When is he –

—   He's not coming back.

ADITYA	How could that happen? Was he not careful at the edge?
—	You could say that.
ADITYA	What do you mean?
—	Just stay away from the edge. It gives people stupid ideas.

17.

LISA in the hotel bar, chatting to a man. The MAN is bringing a drink for LISA.

LISA	How long have you been working in construction? And has it always been here in Dubai?
MAN	You ask a lot of questions Lisa. You did say your name was Lisa didn't you?
LISA	Yes.
MAN	I can't believe you're this interested in building sites?
LISA	No I am I –
MAN	But you don't work in –
LISA	No I work in er pharmaceuticals. Really boring.
MAN	Trust me my job is not that interesting either. You're out here for work right?
LISA	Yes.
MAN	Been here for a while?
LISA	A few weeks. Trying to make contacts.
MAN	How's it going?

LISA	Not that well to be honest. I've spoken to a lot of people, well tried to, but I have just got nothing. Anyway. I don't believe your job is all boring. All these projects you have here. These amazing towers. I love the scale of these skyscrapers. They seem impossible.
MAN	Yes no to be fair. That is the best bit of the job, looking up at these buildings and thinking I helped make that.
LISA	Do you get to go and visit the sites?
MAN	Sometimes.
LISA	And do you work for a company or freelance or …?
MAN	A company called SkyLine. You won't have heard of them.
LISA	No I think I have.

18.

ANDY and DEBBIE's house. DEBBIE has the print out.

DEBBIE	Andy? Is this yours?
ANDY	What?
DEBBIE	Did you print this?
ANDY	Not that I can think of.
DEBBIE	This was sitting on top of the printer.
ANDY	Let me see. Oh yeah. It's the logo for that building company. I did print this ages ago.
DEBBIE	How come?
ANDY	I can't even …
DEBBIE	We work for this company.

ANDY	Really?
DEBBIE	Yeah. We've been doing the communications for their London projects. We're up for a massive contract with them, I mean like huge. That's what I've been working on. The money is crazy.
ANDY	Brilliant.
DEBBIE	And if I get this contract then we'll be sorted.
ANDY	What do you mean?
DEBBIE	Yeah, I'd be taking a lead on the account, so it's like a proper pay rise. You could be a stay-at-home dad if you want. Make the dinner every night. Look after Sophie. Which reminds me, I've got Sophie's Headteacher to meet us on Friday afternoon.
ANDY	Nice one. I'll put it in the calendar.

19.

| ADITYA | It's cold when the sun goes down but still some nights we have to sleep on top of the skyscraper. Easier than getting us back to the camp. It's getting higher. Ten thousand feet and climbing. Twenty thousand feet. It's cold. |

Plane sound effects.

Phone call.

| SALMA | Yeah. Adhi that sounds great. Tallest building in the Gulf. Amazing. |
| ADITYA | Like something from the future. Last stop between here and space. |

SALMA	Right Adhi. Humey paisey chahiye.
ADITYA	…
SALMA	Aap ney suni meri baat?
ADITYA	Yes.
SALMA	It's been months.
ADITYA	I know and I'm.
SALMA	No Addy. We don't have the shop anymore. We need some of this money.
ADITYA	And I'm sending it, I am but –
SALMA	Nahin Adhi. Humary pass kuch nahin raha.
ADITYA	It's complicated. It's coming. I promise.
SALMA	Don't promise just. Just tell me what is –
ADITYA	I've got to go.
SALMA	No no Adhi you –
ADITYA	I've got to go.
ADITYA	Lots of people die here. It wasn't just Ahmed. They walk off the top of the buildings as we work. One moment he is there. Then he is a smudge on the ground at the foot of the tower. His brains in a puddle around him. It happens a lot. A man falls. And another, and another.

And after they die. They follow me. They don't have faces and their skin is grey and still they look at me and they follow me. They want me to join them. They want me to fall off the edge. I stand on the unfinished sixty third floor, open to the sky and I feel their soft dead hands gently |

pushing on my back. I don't know how to get rid of them.

Back at the camp I see a man sometimes. His hair is thick and black and he wears sunglasses.

I see him with his arm around a man like me. He smiles and his teeth dazzle and he is gone.

I try to keep hold of the facts to push away the dead men.

The name of my Father. The colour of the walls at home. The …

I wait to black out but it doesn't happen.

So I step outside the hut and try to breathe the sky into my lungs.

The man with the sunglasses.

AGENT   You want to get out of here?

ADITYA   Yes.

AGENT   There is a way. I mean it. There is a way. For a small fee. Plans of the Airport. Time of the flight. A hatch into the luggage compartment.

ADITYA   And the next day I realise what was our story is now their story.

With hope in my pocket, I am no longer one of the ghosts.

I stand on top of the glass monster and look out across the city.

My senses are sharpened. Those grey men don't have their hands on me anymore.

I will get out of here. I am one of the lucky ones.

An almost imperceptible breeze loosens the sweat above my eyebrows and as a bead rolls down my hairline, I imagine where I will be in a few weeks.

And so days and nights accelerate until I'm here for the last time, sat on the roof of the unfinished building. Tonight we sleep up here. Blinking lights below and the stars just out of reach. The moon nods to me. He understands my endeavours.

Those little things start to return. The smell of fish cooked over coals. My father's gentle chuckle as he teases my mother. My sister's hand resting on her hip in an attempt to be serious. The grey men tumble off the edge, but I'm looking up.

20.

LISA is part of a small party who are being taken around a half-built scyscraper.

GUIDE   So you'll see here the remarkable vista stretching right out across the Gulf. And sadly we can't go up to the very top but if you follow me round this corner …

MAN   What is it going to be called?

GUIDE   We are at the moment in discussion with our really exciting corporate partners about what to call the building. A lot of locals have taken to calling it "The Spaceport" because of the retro futuristic design, and of course, the height.

It will be the tallest building in the Middle East, so of course the name will reflect that as well as the support of our fantastic investment partners. Mind your step.

And here we are. Look out across all that space. So majestic and I think, very peaceful. A wonderful space for people to reflect and be proud of this building. That's really important to all our corporate partners, that everyone feels included. We're all part of one family.

LISA   Really?

GUIDE   Absolutely.

LISA   The construction workers are they part of the family too?

GUIDE   What do you mean?

LISA   What does it actually mean to be 'part of the family'. Long term employment?

GUIDE   Well. A lot of them are on temporary contracts.

LISA   Right.

GUIDE   I mean they are hired through different contractors. It's complicated.

LISA   Not that complicated. I'm just asking what the terms of their employment are. What's the long term –

GUIDE   Well negotiations take place between the architects and the local authorities and construction firms and so their long term, erm, it's really no one person's responsibility …

LISA   So who is looking after their welfare?

GUIDE	What is it you're wanting to –
LISA	The conditions I imagine could be dangerous, so do they get training or –?
GUIDE	I can assure you everyone is treated with the greatest of –
LISA	Can we talk to them?
GUIDE	What?
LISA	Can we talk to the workers?
GUIDE	Sorry, Lisa wasn't it? We could maybe have a chat at the end of this –
LISA	Him there. Hello?

21.

ADITYA	And so the day comes. I am leaving.
LISA	Can we talk to that man, can we talk to him?
—	Please if you would rejoin the group please Lisa.
ADITYA	This is the day I escape.

ADITYA/The MAN moves out of sight.

LISA looks at where he was. She rejoins the group.

—	We need to go now. If you could all follow me back to the lift that would be great.

22.

DEBBIE and ANDY are in the office of the HEADTEACHER, who we don't see but her voice comes from the microphone upstage.

DEBBIE	So you promise you'll back me up?

ANDY	Of course.
DEBBIE	Just every time on the phone she's all soft and nice and then when I hang up I realise that she's only being nice to get rid of me.
ANDY	Well look we're here now. So we'll get something sorted. She knows Sophie needs help, she agrees with that.
DEBBIE	Just don't go soft on me OK?
ANDY	OK.

HEADTEACHER enters.

HEADTEACHER	Sorry to keep you waiting.
DEBBIE	That's OK, thanks for meeting us.
HEAD	Debbie isn't it?
DEBBIE	Yes and this is my husband Andy.
HEADTEACHER	I remember.
ANDY	Hi.
HEADTEACHER	So. Let's talk about Sophie. She is a really sensitive soul isn't she?
DEBBIE	Is she?
HEADTEACHER	Absolutely, she's thoughtful and, er considered.
DEBBIE	And really struggling with her work.
HEADTEACHER	Right.

ANDY's phone rings.

| ANDY | Sorry I'll just er … |

He sends it to voicemail.

| DEBBIE | Did you turn it off? |

ANDY   Yeah of course.

DEBBIE   OK. Look it's not just the work. It's
                everything. She can't make friends. She's
                scared of the teachers. Something has to
                change.

23.

LISA at Departure Lounge. LISA at Dubai Airport, on the phone to ANDY.

*Hi. This is ANDY FIELDING. Sorry I can't take your call right now.
Leave me a message and I'll get back to you soon as I can.*

LISA   Andy it's Lisa. I. I was going to say. I don't
                know what I was going to say. Sorry.

   She hangs up the phone.

   Her phone rings.

LISA   Andy?

AGENT   Hi Lisa, it's me, do you have a minute to
                chat through what you want me to say to
                the publishers?

LISA   Can we talk when I get back?

AGENT   Just a few minutes. They need a bit of
                placating – it's all fine – but now you're
                holding off the next book in the series,
                I need to get back with some sort of
                timescale.

LISA   No but I'm on my way home now.

AGENT   Oh isn't your flight next week –

LISA   I changed it.

AGENT   Everything OK?

LISA   Yeah. Good. It's been really good and
                interesting.

AGENT	Great.
LISA	And I think I've. You know met some interesting people and …
AGENT	So it's feeling …
LISA	Well it's complicated isn't it? I mean I didn't think I was going to solve anything, or you know uncover some great truth. I really don't know what exactly I was going to do.
AGENT	No of course.
LISA	Yeah. I've not been sleeping actually and just feel like I've sort of humiliated myself.
AGENT	I'm sure you haven't.
LISA	Whatever I just. I am coming home, and I'm just going to pick up where I left off and write the next Greyforest book.
AGENT	That's great.
LISA	Yep. Another nice cosy murder book.
AGENT	Well, as long as you're happy to –
LISA	Yeah. It's. Listen I think my flight is being called.
AGENT	Of course.
LISA	Yeah that's the final boarding call so I should –
AGENT	Absolutely. Call me when you're back and up for talking. I think what you've done is great Lisa, you're a wonderful writer with a real gift and –
LISA	Thanks that's … Sorry I've got to go. Bye.

LISA waits. Her flight is some time away. There is a TV in the lounge, she looks up at it. The words are spoken into an onstage microphone by one of the ensemble.

| — | Only days to go now until the launch of India's mission to Mars. The eyes of the world are on the Mangalyaan one as we ask, will they be the first country in history to have a successful maiden voyage to the Red Planet? |

24.

ADITYA on the Airfield. Phone call.

ADITYA	I walk across a patch of scrubland. I look at the bright blue sky, and the planes flying away to somewhere better.
SALMA	Adhi?
ADITYA	Yes,
SALMA	Addy, what the. Where have you been? We haven't heard from you in weeks. What is −?
ADITYA	It's going to be OK, Salma. We're going to be OK.
SALMA	What do you −?
ADITYA	I've got it sorted now. I've found a way. I worked out the trick.
SALMA	What trick, Adhi? What are you talking about?
ADITYA	The trick Salma. I worked it out. I found the corner. Where I can reach my hand in. You see?

SALMA	No Adhi, mujhy kuch dikhai nahin de raha. I don't know what you're talking about.
ADITYA	It swarms and rushes but I know how to get it.
SALMA	Adhi, you're talking like …
ADITYA	I know. Don't worry Salma.
SALMA	I am worried. You sound like a mad –
ADITYA	It wasn't OK for a while, I can say that now but it will be. It's fine now, it's going to be incredible, Salma. We're gonna be rich.
SALMA	I don't want to be rich, I just. What are you saying, Adhi?
ADITYA	I'm saying. I'm saying.
SALMA	Adhi?
ADITYA	I'm saying that.
SALMA	Adhi please.
ADITYA	Salma?
SALMA	Adhi?
ADITYA	It's going to be OK, Salma. Tell Mum and Dad. It's going to be OK.
SALMA	Adhi? Adhi? What is going on?
ADITYA	I'm at the edge of the airfield. The chainlink fence. Main taiyar hoon. I put on the final layers of clothes, like the man said. There is a hole under the fence, like the man said.

25.

DEBBIE	But she isn't coping, why would you say that? She is getting lost in that class.

67

HEADTEACHER	I wouldn't use –
DEBBIE	She can never do the reading. If I even mention it she practically bursts into tears.
HEADTEACHER	I know but.
DEBBIE	Her reading age is way below the rest of the –
HEADTEACHER	Those things are always a guideline.
DEBBIE	Yes but she's miles behind everyone.
HEADTEACHER	I wish I could do something more.
DEBBIE	Then do something. Why can't you get a teaching assistant to help her? You say you recognise how bad her dyslexia is but –
HEADTEACHER	I've told you we can't afford –
DEBBIE	How come you can you afford translators then?
HEADTEACHER	Well.
DEBBIE	For every kid that turns up. Half of them barely stay a term before they disappear.
HEADTEACHER	It's quite complicated.
DEBBIE	You say that. But. Look I'm not. I want all the kids to have a fair chance. But we've been living here for twelve years and we stayed here because of this school and you're not prepared to just help us even a little bit.
HEADTEACHER	…

ANDY's phone rings again.

ANDY	Sorry I thought I'd turned that off.
DEBBIE	Just answer it.

ANDY answers and walks out.

ANDY	Hello?
LISA	Oh. Andy.
ANDY	Yes. It is.
LISA	It's Lisa. Lisa from.
ANDY	Yeah yeah I.
LISA	I was expecting your voicemail. I had stuff all thought out.
ANDY	Are you OK?
LISA	I'm in Dubai.
ANDY	Dubai?
LISA	Yes I. You were right Andy. So well done. I don't know what I was chasing. I don't know what I'm doing. It's just endless sand and fucking glass everywhere. I didn't solve this, whatever 'this' is. I didn't do anything. Like you said. I should have mailed a bloody cheque to Comic Relief and got over myself. You were right.
ANDY	I don't know.
LISA	Well anyway. It's over now.
ANDY	Is it?
LISA	Look I've tried. Every path I go down is so overwhelming he gets swallowed up by, jargon and bureaucracy and complex chains of ownership and documentation and –
ANDY	But it is just him isn't it? On his own. In the sky.
LISA	What?

ANDY	I mean that's the thing, you imagine him dying, totally alone and think, that can't be the end. He can't just be gone and that's the end of it.
LISA	So what do I write?
ANDY	I guess you just have to try and see what happens.
LISA	I have tried and. I wish this had gone to voicemail.
ANDY	Sorry.
LISA	No I am. I have to get on my plane.
ADITYA	I'm walking towards the terminal, looking for something I recognise from the drawings the man gave me.
	I can see the Boeing 747, that will be heading to London. Just like the man said. I walk towards it.

26.

Sequence of both LISA and ADITYA trying to get onto the plane. She is at the check-in desk, queueing at the gate and so on. He is clambering in and around the chairs, the scaffolding, the other bodies.

LISA stands on ADITYA to get to her seat and in an impossible moment, sees him fleetingly in front of her. She sits in her plane seat, and he is crushed under her feet. ADITYA appears again, floating in front of her.

LISA	And there he is. Under the plane. Clinging on to the inside of the underbelly. He looks down the massive metal leg, at the concrete of the runway twelve feet below. He has to get ready for take off.
	He looks for the hatch into the luggage compartment. His eyes and fingers search

desperately. There is no hatch. Of course not. He can't believe he actually thought that was true.

Still. He can stay here. He needs to get himself into a position so he doesn't get crushed when the wheels fold in.

27.

LISA

As the plane starts to move, he tenses his whole body so as not to fall out. The plane tears along the runway, his body rattles and jolts as the plane lifts off and the wheels fold up, sealing him in.

Colossal Sound of a plane taking off.

The engines are a wall of sound pushing against him. He is swallowed by a heavy cloud of heat. His face is centimetres away from the tyre. The smell of hot rubber and petrol fumes.

The plane has taken off, He is alive and flying.

The other passengers are now SALMA and ANDY, but they also still represent bodies on the plane.

SALMA

It's me again. I don't know if you're listening to these voicemails but please just. Let me know you're OK.

LISA

Zero degrees and climbing into colder air. Ten thousand feet, minus ten. Twenty thousand feet, minus twenty. Thirty thousand feet, minus thirty.

His lungs are flimsy. Tiny plastic bags. It is hard to determine when he is asleep or awake.

71

Occasionally a wave of blinding pain flashes through him. He is experiencing hypoxia, a severe lack of oxygen to the brain. His skin has blisters and his eyes are flooded with an icy white light. The hypoxia causes him to hallucinate. Memories and images collide in his head. The bolts and rivets reveal the faces of his family. The tyre is a peaceful night sky.

SALMA   Whatever has happened it doesn't matter.

LISA   The cold is sneaking into every cell of his body.

SALMA   Whatever you've done we'll work it out. Don't worry about money or anything.

LISA   His mind has turned to ice.

SALMA   Sub Kuch theek hai.

LISA   And his thoughts are skidding across the surface.

SALMA   Just come home.

LISA   One idea cracks through and sinks down into his belly.

ADITYA   I think I might be dying.

SALMA   I go to the beach Adhi, and look out to the sea. And that way I can hear you.

LISA   He is dead. His body is frozen. Covered in a thin layer of ice.

The other passengers are asleep on the plane.

LISA   The pilot flicks a switch to release the landing gear, it goes from amber to red. The wheels curl out of the belly of the plane.

His frozen body falls out and into the sky.
Cuts through the blue clear day and the ice
melts a little during the descent.

He is a golden shard which pierces through
the roof of the sky and out into the infinity
of black space.

His body lands in the car park of a DIY
superstore in an affluent suburb of London.

And from where he lies a tiny hairline
crack zigs zags out his mouth.

EPILOGUE

28.

ANDY in the garden. LISA is at the book festival reading.

LISA   A year after he found the body. Andy is
       sitting in his garden.

       He has a cold beer.

       He has the paper.

       He looks at the grass growing and the
       flowers ambling in the wind.

       He sees an article about a Lorry full of dead
       migrants which was found abandoned in a
       layby off the M62.

       The image is blurry but you can see a pile
       of dead bodies.

       And every single body has the face of the
       Stowaway he saw in the B&Q car park.

       He shakes the image.

       He thinks – the world's a royal fucking mess.

His family will be home soon.

He goes to get another beer.

Sit in the sunshine.

They'll be home soon.

LISA finishes reading from the book.

HOST   Thanks so much for that reading from your book. It's not been without controversy this book has it?

LISA   I guess not.

HOST   What made you think you should tell this story? What really sparked it off?

LISA   Well it was sort of a surprise to me.
I was planning to do the next one in the 8 series, that world I'd been in for some time, but then this thing happened to me, I was there, I couldn't just –

HOST   Let me rephrase the question, because of course we know that you were there, you were physically near when the tragic incident happened but, what gives you a connection to it? What made you think *you* could tell this story?

LISA   Sorry?

HOST   You're a privileged white woman, what made you think you were the one to tell it?

LISA   I er. I just thought I had to try. At least try and tell it. That felt the right thing to do.

HOST   The right thing to do. That's an interesting choice of phrase.

LISA   Maybe but …

| HOST | I'm going to open that out to the audience I'm interested in this notion of an author 'doing the right thing'. Anyone like to speak about that? |

HOST notices a man with his hand up.

ANDY	Hi. It's Andy from the book.
HOST	Ok, there we go. That was one of my questions, if there was any truth in the Andy story?
ANDY	Yeah it's true, all the stuff that happened to me but still I think. I mean I liked the book but I think the way you write about me, it's not. I don't think you've got me right.
HOST	In a bad way?
ANDY	Well. No but.
LISA	I wasn't trying to make you look bad. I don't think he does. I think 'Andy', as a character, needs to get on with his life.
HOST	Andy 'the character'?
LISA	Yes. Well it's made up.
HOST	But you know him.
LISA	Yeah but I. I only know what I know of him. And what I see.
HOST	So you're saying it's only part of the story. Only one take on it?
LISA	Of course it's only one take. That's all you ever get. You try and fold all these different voices and facts and things you've imagined, and it's all just stories that you're weaving. But sometimes all we have are

stories. And you need to collect as many of them as you can.

He died, on his own, in the middle of a flight. And I thought, it can't just end there. That can't be the end of his story.

We still don't know who he was, where he came from. The only identifying feature was a jacket with a logo on it. The logo of a company that refuse to acknowledge the existence of this man. He hasn't even been buried. I wanted him to be remembered. And not as a anonymous body in a car park but as human being with desires, not so different from mine. But because he was born into one story and I was born into another, his life ended the way it did. And mine, well, mine led here.

HOST   Do you have any regrets writing this book?

LISA   Well I regret that I had to write it. But I did and now we're having this conversation so we have to look at it, however difficult, we have to look at this man who tried to smuggle himself into this country and before that the impossibly hard journey he made, and before that the awful circumstances that made him take the journey, and before that he was just a little boy, who would run and play and just be a little boy.

29.

The sound of planes.

ADITYA and SALMA on the beach picking up things which they could sell.

ADITYA	One day. Do you think everything will be better Salma?
SALMA	What do you mean?
ADITYA	Well like. Will like everyone be rich and happy and live in big houses?
SALMA	What are you talking about?
ADITYA	I just think about the future and what it will look like.
SALMA	You are so weird sometimes. What's that you've found?
ADITYA	Sim card.
SALMA	Put it in your pocket.
ADITYA	I just. I mean like if we work really hard then maybe Dad wouldn't do that thing where he goes outside to cry and then pretends he didn't. You know we'd just have more stuff and I mean you know things will get better, won't they?
SALMA	Things are fine. Come on. Help me with this we've got to get back to Dad at the shop.
ADITYA	I'll race you, ten, nine, eight, go!
SALMA	What?!! Wait!
ADITYA	Come on! Faster faster! You can't catch me! You can't catch me!

ANNOUNCEMENT:

> The anticipation is really building here today as a whole nation, indeed people of every nations turn their gaze skyward, to see if this will be a successful takeoff, and indeed what new discoveries may be made as this rocket prepares for its journey into outer space.

Recorded voiceover begins.

ADITYA begins to rise off the ground. People gather to watch the launch of the mission to mars. Countdown. They move in to help ADITYA climb, and in turn they too climb. The company watch him fly away. The lights go down.

Blackout.

WWW.OBERONBOOKS.COM